My Favorite Garden

My Favorite Garden

Written By: Journei Jewel and Kandice Green

Illustrations by Robert Paul Jr.

Printed in the United States of America

ISBN-978-0-578-70042-7

Journei Green, a book lover and
first-time author, has teamed
up with her mom to present her
imagination on illustrated paper.
She enjoys dance, gymnastics and
learning new things to show her
two younger sisters. Spending
time at school is where she began
to think of becoming an author
and having a book of her own.
After her father passed away
when she was only 3 years old,
she wanted to make something
special to help other kids
deal with that kind of pain.
The best thing to do is
remain full of love and hope,
even when she felt like crying.
Believing she could be many

Dedicated to all the children who have lost someone they love!!

"Every morning, I count the painted clouds like giant daisies that are reaching for the sky..."

"The best time to dream about anything is while you are awake. . .. That way, whatever you may think of is possible!" She told her two sisters.

"I'm pretending to be a flower fairy with soft, pink and purple wings. Look at me, flying through the wind like a perfect butterfly."

"I will make it rain with my magic mind and flood the air with beautiful pedals that will shower us forever. . .."

"I find so much comfort on this grass. Just imagine sleeping on a soft pile of purple pansies."

"What are pansies? They sound really yummy! Can I eat them?" Her baby sister asked.

"Ha ha, that's funny! No silly, it is a garden flower that stands for thought or too remember! Every flower means something." Journei answered.

"Come on! Follow me and we will visit a field full of my favorite flowers." They each ran off to explore.

"This is the quiet place where our loved ones lay to rest before they go to Heaven."

"I believe that if you miss someone who lives beyond the sky, there will always be a way to reach them."

"Here, hold this Dandelion. . . I call this one a wishing stick!"
They each held up their fluffy flower.

"Now, keep your eyes closed! Whisper your wishes to the wind, then take a deep breath and blow!" They did just as she said.

"This will send our prayer past the clouds. Trust me! Faith means we must have hope, even if you do not see it yet!"

"Did you know that God loved the world so much that he gave his only Son to us?" She yelled out.

"He hears when we pray, and He knows our heart. All we have to do is believe in Him!"

"Check out this crossroad, these are called memory lane, every garden has a path or two."

"We were created to bloom like a tiny rose in his garden. Each being different. . . some tall or short, even big or small."

"One day, we will grow until we can't grow anymore! When he picks us. . . then shall we meet in Heaven to live with him!"

"My Father's House has many rooms, if it were not true, I would not tell you it is so. He went to prepare a place."

"How amazing it must be to live in peace forever, protected by God for life... That's why it's my Favorite."

Fun **FACT**:: The name pansy is from the French word pensie, meaning thought or remembrance.

A Daughter's Note

Hey Daddy,

I have flowers for you today

just to keep your garden pretty.

One magnolia with Blue roses,

daffodils and a white lily.

I know that Heaven will hold a place

so I could be next to you. . .

It hurts that you have gone away

but prayers help me through.

I promise to keep your memory alive

and leave my love at the stone.

Still forever daddy's girl

I really miss you, Jerome!

JOSHUA
JEROME
GREEN
"GATOR"

#TruKing   1·13·84 - 5·11·15

Loving Son, Brother, Husband,
Father, Family Friend...
Until We Meet Again

"We are confident, I say, and willing
rather to be absent from the body, and
to be present with the Lord."
2 Corinthians 5:8

Welcome To

In Loving Memory Joshua Jerome Green

1-13-84 * 5-11-15

Hebrew 11:1

John 3:16

John 14:2

www.ingramcontent.com/pod-product-compliance
Lightning Source LLC
LaVergne TN
LVHW072053070426
835508LV00002B/76